# THE LITTLE BOOK ON RELATIONSHIPS:
## Have Happier Relationships by Understanding People's Colour Personality Types

Beverly Kepple

# THE LITTLE BOOK ON RELATIONSHIPS

© 2017 by Beverly Kepple

ISBN 978-0-9567195-3-9

# DEDICATION

To Lindsay and our ever-increasing family, who inspire me, encourage me and make me so very happy.

# TABLE OF CONTENTS

# 1. WHY READ THIS BOOK?

Do you ever get angry or frustrated with someone else? Does the person say things that irritate you? Or do they say things that upset you?

Do some people make you so mad you want to scream or shout? Or perhaps people shout at you?

Do you wish they didn't talk so much ……or talk more?

Do you share your feelings with others or keep them hidden?

Do you just "click" with some people? You get on really well but you are not sure why?

These are typical reactions because people behave in different ways. We think differently. We talk differently. Our life experiences are quite different.

The number of relationships each of us has is huge. There's your partner, husband, wife, children, friends, neighbours, boss or work colleagues, so it's not surprising that there are issues at times.

If you are reading this book it's probably because you want at least one of your relationships to improve, to be happier or more satisfying. The key to great relationships is recognizing different personalities and understanding human behaviour. Why we do certain things, why we don't do others. Why something is amusing to one person but not to another. Why some actions irritate us whereas other actions are acceptable.

Every human is unique …. that's what makes us human. But there are certain characteristics of our personality or behaviour that are common and when we recognise these we become more understanding, more tolerant of each other. Relationships improve.

The most important thing to understand is your own behaviour. Knowing is not enough. We need to recognise certain ways of behaving and know when we need to change that. If you develop an interest in learning more about yourself and about other people, you'll be amazed at the insights you get. If you put into practice the information in this book you WILL have happier relationships.

This book teaches and uses a model based on the theory that there are 4 different types of personalities. Four different ways people can behave in response to something.

At this stage, you might be thinking "I'll skip the next chapter and read the interesting ones on relationships"

Please don't.

*The next chapter* is the key to it all.

# 2. THE KEY TO PERSONALITY TYPES

Way back in 400BC Hippocrates noticed that people showed one of four characteristic types of behaviour which he gave the names of bodily fluids.

Yellow Bile or Choleric
Blood or Sanguine
Phlegm or Phlegmatic
Black Bile or Melancholic.

Since then, lots of different models that describe the 4 types of behaviour or personalities have been developed.

**Animals**: Lion, Otter, Retriever and Beaver

**Birds**: Eagle, Peacock, Dove and Owl

**DISC Model:** Dominance, Influence, Steadiness and Compliance

**Colours**: Red, Yellow, Green & Blue

**Physical Elements**: Fire, Air, Water & Earth

***People* Model:** *Powerful, Popular, Peaceful and Perfect*

It doesn't matter what name is given to the personality types, they are all the same and each has its own characteristics.

We behave in a way that is a mixture of these 4 types or styles. It's a unique mixture. Everyone is different. But everyone has one or two and occasionally three of these that are stronger than the others and therefore this type of behaviour is the one that occurs more than the others.

In this book, we will use Colours and the People model to explain personality types.

### Powerful Red Personality
*Powerful Red People* are assertive, driving, competitive and ambitious. Their driving force or motivation is to be in control, to feel *Powerful*.

### Popular Yellow Personality
*Popular Yellow People* are talkative, friendly, sociable and enthusiastic. Their driving force or motivation is to be *Popular* and liked by everyone.

### Peaceful Green Personality
*Peaceful Green People* are calm, loyal and patient. Their driving force or motivation is for steadiness, everything to remain the same, for their life to be *Peaceful*.

### Perfect Blue Personality
*Perfect Blue People* are Perfectionists. It's not that they think they are Perfect, it's just that they have very high standards. They are accurate, analytical, conscientious, and cautious.

Which is your main personality type?

Can you pick it from the descriptions above?

In each of my books I take you through the following exercise to create your Personality Tool to use in the future. You'll need a piece of paper or cardboard to write on.

Are you louder and outgoing (*Powerful Red* or *Popular Yellow styles*) or more reserved and quieter (*Peaceful Green* or *Perfect Blue* styles)?

On your piece of paper or card draw a vertical line in the middle of the page. Write **out-going and louder** at the top. Write **reserved and quieter** on the bottom. This line is a continuum, a continuous change from outgoing to reserved behaviour. The nearer to the top of the line then the more outgoing you are. Nearer the bottom, the more reserved you are. Where do you lie on the line? Place a cross or point on the line.

To help you decide think about when you are with a group of people. Do you like to get up and talk to everyone in the room (outgoing) or do you prefer to observe the others and just talk to the ones you know (reserved)?

Now if you are saying to yourself, "well sometimes I am outgoing and sometimes I'm not", then that may be true in different situations but you can't be outgoing and reserved at the same time, so think about what you mostly are and mark the vertical line.

For instance, a person can be trained and practice enough so that they are a dynamic and entertaining speaker on stage (outgoing), but off the stage they may be quiet and reserved. Their behaviour is what they do for that given situation. Think about yourself when you are relaxed at home, or with your friends.

On the same piece of paper and in the middle of the page draw a horizontal line. On the left write **task-focused** and on the right side write **people-focused**. This line is a continuum from task-focused to people-focused behaviour. On the left we have people who focus on tasks whereas on the right we have people who focus on people.

Your Personality Tool should now look like this.

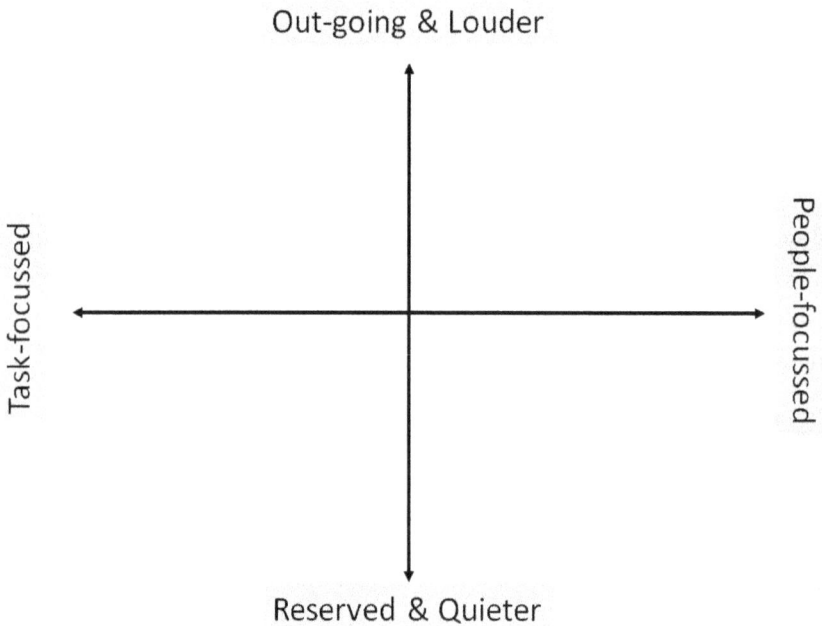

Out-going & Louder

Task-focussed

People-focussed

Reserved & Quieter

What do you talk about mostly…. your work or your family? Your hobby or sport or the friends you do it with? Where do you lie on that line? Put a cross or point on that spot.

For instance, when you come back from a holiday do you tell everyone about the places, restaurants or activities (task-focused) or do you talk about the people you went with or the people you met (people-focused)?

Choose the side that you are most like.

It's often best to get a close friend, partner, someone who knows you well, to cross check your opinion as to where you place your crosses. They are likely to be less biased.

If you look at your page you should have four quadrants.

In the top left quadrant write *POWERFUL RED*

In the top right quadrant write *POPULAR YELLOW*

In the bottom right quadrant write *PEACEFUL GREEN*

In the bottom left quadrant write *PERFECT BLUE*

You now have 2 points on your diagram, lying on the axes of one of the quadrants as in this example.

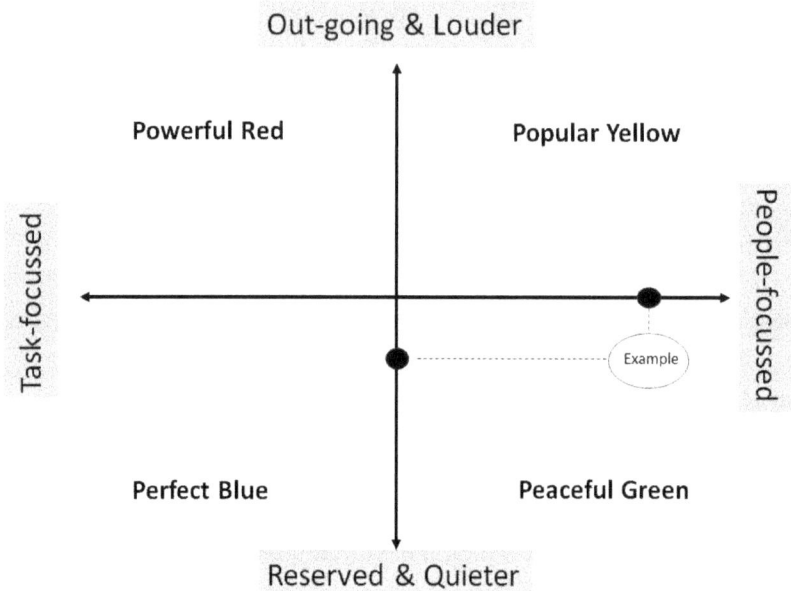

Out-going & Louder

Powerful Red          Popular Yellow

Task-focussed          People-focussed

Example

Perfect Blue          Peaceful Green

Reserved & Quieter

This describes your main personality style. This is how other people see you. Let me reassure you that there is no right or wrong, no better or worse quadrant; it's just the main style of personality that other people observe from you most of the time.

Each quadrant or Personality Type has its own characteristics. How you behave in a situation depends on your Main Type... Write the following descriptions in the appropriate quadrant.

***POWERFUL RED* (Top left)**
Direct, Assertive, Ambitious and Competitive

***POPULAR YELLOW* (Top right)**
Sociable, Friendly, Enthusiastic and Talkative

***PEACEFUL GREEN* (Lower right)**
Calm, Steady, Patient and Loyal

***PERFECT BLUE* (Lower left)**
Precise, Accurate, Cautious with high standards


You have now created your ***Personality Tool***. Keep this page as you will want to refer to it frequently.

If you are someone in the ***Powerful Red*** quadrant you need to feel you are in control, because you like to feel *Powerful*. You are direct in dealing with others, assertive, ambitious and quite competitive in all things from competing in a sports event, winning a board game with your youngster to completing a project ahead of others at work.

If you are in the ***Popular Yellow*** quadrant, you want to feel *Popular* so you like to be around people. You are a friendly, sociable person, always enthusiastic and you love to talk. At any event, be that a family gathering or a work-related networking event, you quickly attract a group of people around you.

If you are in the ***Peaceful Green*** quadrant you like security. You prefer a *Peaceful* environment and dislike sudden change. You remain calm at all times, steady, patient and extremely loyal. You are always there for you family and friends with little kindnesses such as thank you notes, remembering birthdays and catch-up phone calls.

If you are in the *Perfect Blue* quadrant you like to get jobs done *Perfectly*. This is true whether you are completing a work project or tidying the kitchen after dinner. You like to have procedures to follow and you produce quality work.

Think about the everyday event of having a meal. How we do this on a regular basis is generally governed by our personality style.

The *Powerful Red* person often eats fast because there are more challenging things to get on with. They are happy to eat alone as they are not particularly interested in social chit chat.

The *Popular Yellow* person prefers to eat with others, chatting, turning it into a social occasion. The more people the better.

The *Peaceful Green* person also prefers to eat with others rather than alone. They will be more concerned with helping the children and making sure everyone has what they want to eat.

The *Perfect Blue* person is happy to eat alone. They are quite precise and particular with what they put on their fork. If in a restaurant they like to read the entire menu before choosing.

# 3. I'M ME AND I'M UNIQUE

Are you having difficulty identifying your own main personality type?

Everybody has some of the characteristics of each of the 4 types but in varying amounts. That's what makes you unique.

The personality that others see comes from your main style. Most People have a combination or blend of two types, sometimes three. If you are having difficulty determining your main type then you are probably a blend and you'll demonstrate characteristics from each of your main styles at different times.

At work you might usually behave in a direct, forceful way with little time for small talk (*Powerful Red*). However, at other times you might stop for a chat and seem quite friendly (*Popular Yellow*). You have 2 main styles.

Another person could be a combination of *Peaceful Green* and *Perfect Blue*, steady, patient and modest but also at times, cautious, accurate and precise.

Two other common combinations are: *Powerful Red* with *Perfect Blue* and *Popular Yellow* with *Peaceful Green*. It is important to remember that the personality you exhibit depends on the situation you are in and the person(s) you are relating to.

For happy relationships, you must first really understand yourself.

Why?

Because you have strong points and you also have limitations. We all do. It is these strengths and limitations that get in the way of a great relationship.

If you work with me through this book you will understand how others see or find you. You will become aware of the aspects of your personality that have an impact on a relationship.

When people argue they usually say the other person said this or did that. They don't think about what they themselves said or did ..... because it's natural to think we're right and the other person is wrong. That's what an argument or disagreement is.

The *Personality* way of looking at the situation is that both people are right but view the situation or issue from a different angle. First understand how you view the world. .... how others see or find you. Then you will understand when you need to make small changes to your behaviour to match the other person so you get on better.

The next four chapters cover the behaviour of each of the four personality styles. At this stage just read your own one. If you have two main styles you'll need to read both of them.

# 4. *POWERFUL RED* PERSONALITY

If this is your main style, this is how you behave and how other people find you ….

**Strengths that you bring to any relationship**

You are strong-willed, strong-minded and want to be a leader of people. You are direct and demanding. You feel you can control or change things around you. You love being in charge, whether that's within your family, at work or in the sport field.

There are no obstacles for you, only challenges to rise to. A risk-taker, you challenge the status quo and don't mind breaking the rules. You are always in a rush, wanting things done now. You live in the present. Never still, on the go always moving around, multi-tasking, you get more done and don't waste a second.

You do not want to be controlled or told what to do. You love it when there are no rules or restrictions placed on you. Motivated by success, money and being powerful, you want the result and you want it now.

As a *Powerful Red Personality,* you speak directly, straight to the point and are not interested in small talk or the details. You may use lots of big hand gestures when you talk. You tell it like it is and you don't mind telling people they are wrong. You are not aware and probably don't care that this might upset others.

Your appearance is important to you. You like to dress to show how successful you are…. we could call it power-dressing. You wear classic designer clothes that are expensive and beautifully made. You will also have expensive jewellery and shoes, and if you are a woman, expensive handbags. These things make you feel good…. feel successful and powerful.

In your family relationships you are the planner, the driver. Not only do you want to be successful, you want your wife, husband, partner and children to be successful too.

In your work relationships, you are assertive and direct; you like to take control, always driving towards new goals with a sense of urgency. You need a variety of work so you don't get bored and you thrive on pressure and a quick moving environment.

**Your limitations…. How you upset or annoy others**

Not everyone has the same drive and urgency as you. They want to conduct their lives at a more measured pace.

Your directness and bluntness can come across as unfriendly or just plain rude to other styles. You get angry quickly and let others know. This can upset other styles.

*Popular Yellow* people can think you are unfriendly.

*Peaceful Green* ones might find you impatient and unapproachable.

*Perfect Blue* people might think you are not thorough enough and skip too many details.

For instance, if your partner's main style is *Popular Yellow* they will want to chat a lot as it helps them feel liked and needed. They like to talk about other people, what everyone said about this and that. But you don't like wasting time with small talk and you aren't really interested in the activities of other people. It's important to the *Popular Yellow* person though. This difference can cause conflict between you both.

If your partner's main style is *Peaceful Green* they need to have reinforced that you love them and appreciate them. They love cards, flowers and being thanked. You don't have the same need as you are a very confident person. They'll get upset if you forget an anniversary and you'll be irritated because you don't see it as that important.

You make decisions easily and quickly but your *Perfect Blue* main style partner doesn't. If you are choosing a holiday destination or buying a house, the *Perfect Blue* partner will research all the details first and analyse the pros and cons before making a decision. They will get very upset if you rush into things. You'll get annoyed at the time they are wasting before coming to a decision.

**In the work environment**

Are you a boss or a manager? Are you aware that because you are a straight talker and blunt, it can upset other personality types at work?

The *Popular Yellow* will think you are unfriendly and that you don't like them.

The *Peaceful Green* can find you intimidating or insensitive and they take it personally. In this situation you will find them withdrawn, uncommunicative.

The *Perfect Blue* will not like your bluntness. This has the effect of making them take even longer over a task to be sure to get it right and avoid criticism from you. They find criticism very hurtful.

The *Powerful Red personality* is always in a hurry. You try to insist on immediate action from others.

The *Popular Yellow* will respond with an overly optimistic opinion of what they can achieve.

The *Peaceful Green* and *Perfect Blue*'s will worry about getting it all done in time and not wanting to be the brunt of your anger if they don't.

# 5. *POPULAR YELLOW* PERSONALITY

If this is your main style, this is how you behave and how other people find you....

**Strengths that you bring to any relationship**

You are fun, enthusiastic and charming. People are naturally attracted to you. You are definitely a people person. You want to help others as this fires up your energy and enthusiasm. Because you can motivate and inspire others, you energise any group you are with, but you also need lots of attention and approval. You need people to like you, to become your friend. You don't like being on your own.

You are talkative. You love telling stories but there is a tendency to exaggerate. Because you are an optimist you tend to over-promise.

You love participating in teams, sharing ideas and entertaining others. This can be in a family group, the work environment or a sport club. You are motivated by having fun, being with people, chatting and telling stories. At any events you are most likely to be surrounded by a crowd who all enjoy your company.

Generally, you wear contemporary clothes, the latest fashions and often bright colours.

**Your limitations…. How you upset or annoy others**

Although you are always enthusiastic and love to talk to people, *Powerful Red* individuals are likely to find you too friendly. You talk too much for their liking. They will think you are wasting too much time on chatter and not getting things done fast enough.

*Peaceful Green* and *Perfect Blue* people will also find you too talkative because they are quieter and not out-going like yourself.

Because you are far more interested in people than things, your bedroom, office and other spaces can look (to others) like a shambles. You know it's a mess with piles of stuff everywhere but it doesn't bother you. You know where everything is. But it will bother the *Powerful Red* and *Perfect Blue*. The *Powerful Red* will think you are inefficient while the mess will really bother the fastidious *Perfect Blue.* This can cause lots of arguments at home.

Although you are a wonderful communicator, you are not a very good listener. Sometimes other people think you try to dominate conversations. This will cause the *Powerful Red* to talk louder and over the top of you, often resulting in an argument. The quieter *Peaceful Green* and *Perfect Blue* will just stop contributing to the conversation. They will be feeling hurt and annoyed. More listening and less talking by you is necessary, particularly when others need to share their ideas.

**In the work environment**

As a manager, you create a collaborative atmosphere and encourage others. As you communicate so easily you love having meetings to openly discuss issues. Remember that other personality types (*Powerful Red* and *Perfect Blue*) would prefer to get on with the work rather than discuss things.

Because you like recognition you are likely to instigate recognition plans for your employees as well as having socials and parties. You also love Team training events. The *Powerful Red* and *Perfect Blue* will not be so enthusiastic. You can win the *Powerful Red* over if they think it will be competitive while the *Perfect Blue* is the ideal person to organize these events for you.

Remember to allow the quieter *Peaceful Green* and *Perfect Blue* members at work to express their point of view, particularly during meetings. Stop talking! Start asking them open-ended questions to help them communicate. The best leaders always ask questions first and save their opinion to last.

You also find it difficult to structure an assignment to delegate to your team because although you are an innovator, you are not a good planner. To help you keep on track you (or one of your *Perfect Blue* members) need to write a plan with target completion dates.

# 6. *Peaceful Green* Personality

If this is your main style, this is how you behave and how other people find you.…

**Strengths that you bring to any relationship**

You are steady and patient. You need and love a consistent familiar environment. You value security. You don't want to take risks or try new things, whether this is a big decision like buying a house or smaller one like shopping in a new store. You respect the way things have always been and therefore you are slow to change.

Motivated by family, friends and everything being calm and peaceful in your environment, you are a great family member, a loyal friend, patient, always sympathetic and supportive. You are always concerned about your family and friends and keeping them happy. You see the world as a place of harmony full of interesting people. You love helping others and working behind the scenes. With any project, you stick to it from start to finish but show modesty in all of your achievements.

Because you are patient and sensitive you are a good listener. You are often known as a peacemaker because you can act as a mediator and reconcile conflicts.

You prefer to wear comfortable, casual clothes. You do not dress to impress others but to create a relaxed feeling for you.

**Your limitations…. How you upset or annoy others**

*Powerful Red* individuals, who love new challenges and do everything at a rapid pace, will think you are too slow and will get annoyed when you don't want something to change. You like a calm relaxed atmosphere. They like urgency and an excited buzz around the place.

*Popular Yellow* people who are loud, out-going and talkative will find you too quiet and modest.

The *Perfect Blue* individual, who concentrates on getting everything done perfectly, might think that you waste too much time being concerned about other people.

You like to feel appreciated for the effort you put into things either at work or at home. A thoughtfully worded thank you card means a lot to you. Just remember that the *Powerful Red* individual is unlikely to thank you. It's just not their way even though they do appreciate you.

You speak softly and when you meet people, especially new people, you like to start with small talk to break the ice. Something to remember though is that you can be overpowered by any *Powerful Red* or *Popular Yellow* people in a conversation. When they start to dominate the discussions, you tend to clam up and not speak.

**In the work environment**

As a manager you are very supportive of the people you manage. You create a pleasant and relaxed atmosphere. People know you are approachable and will listen attentively to any issues.

Being faster-paced, the ***Powerful Red*** and ***Popular Yellow*** may get frustrated with you because things don't move quickly enough for them. You take your time when considering any change in organisation or detail.

# 7. *PERFECT BLUE* PERSONALITY

If this is your main style, this is how you behave and how other people find you....

**Strengths that you bring to any relationship**

You are conscientious and cautious. You like to do things right. You research any decision-making idea thoroughly considering all angles before making a decision.

You love details. You read all the brochures when you buy something. You study the facts and figures and read the small print before committing to anything. To get all the details you need, you will ask lots of questions.

You want to be known for being accurate and logical but you do need time to think. You are a long-term thinker. You find it difficult to give answers on the spot. You hate being rushed and actually prefer to work alone so you can think, plan, prepare, evaluate and problem solve before sharing the material with others. Privacy is very important to you. However, you also work well in small groups with close relationships.

Stopping a task half way through is unacceptable to you. At work, tasks need to be clearly outlined. You like systems and procedures that produce predictable and consistent outcomes. At home, you'll develop routines that make the household run smoothly.

Always smartly dressed you like to look immaculately groomed although you don't feel the need to buy expensive clothing like the *Powerful Red*. Nor are your clothes as bright as the *Popular Yellow*.

Your space (kitchen, bedroom, office, desk, garage etc) is ordered and functional with everything in its place. Before the end of your day your space will be tidied and readied for the next day. You expect others to do the same and find the untidiness of some of the other styles very frustrating.

**Your limitations…. How you upset or annoy others**

There is a tendency to remember the way things were, how you used to do things. This is because you view the world in a cautious and contemplative way. You can be a bit sceptical. You tend to look out for what could go wrong. The optimistic *Powerful Red* and *Popular Yellow* will find this annoying. *Popular Yellow* with their bubbly optimism will think you are pessimistic and far too conservative.

You take a long time to open up to people so when you meet someone for the first time you can seem quite cold. If sitting, you might cross your arms in front of you providing a barrier between you and others, blocking the person out until you get to know them. The *Peaceful Green* may feel hurt and think you aren't interested in them.

Because you strive for perfection in all things you undertake you also expect Perfection from others. This can be quite hard on family members, work colleagues or employees who can't live up to your expectations. *Powerful Red* people with their urgency for completion will get annoyed and think you pay too much attention to detail and don't get on with things fast enough.

You also have a tendency to overload yourself with work. This is because you find it difficult to delegate and will often "do it yourself to make sure it's done right"

## In the work environment

As a manager you are concerned with quality and accuracy so you have high expectation of others. You will expect the systems you have put in place to be followed exactly and this won't always happen.

*Powerful Red* individuals want results as soon as possible and may cut corners to achieve that.

*Popular Yellow* wants work to be fun and they don't like a lot of details.

*Peaceful Green* will do everything you ask of them but it is important to make them feel appreciated

# 8. So What Now?

Having read all about yourself you now need to understand the people in your life. How do you identify their main style?

You can use the *Personality Tool -* you made earlier. Ask yourself two questions. Is the person usually loud and out-going (*Powerful Red* or *Popular Yellow*) ......? or quieter and reserved (*Peaceful Green* or *Perfect Blue*)?

Think about the pace of their voice.... is it loud, lively, forceful, with very few pauses and does it sound self-assured? Then their main style is most likely to be *Powerful Red* or *Popular Yellow*.......... Or is it softly spoken, with longer pauses, does it seem uncertain and does it sound cooperative? Then their main style is *Peaceful Green* or *Perfect Blue*.

What does the person usually talk about most? People tend to talk about either people or other things. If the person talks to you about their work, car, things they have and do, then they are more task-focused and have a lot of *Powerful Red* and/or *Perfect Blue* style. Whereas if they talk to you about their family, friends, employees or other people they know then they are people-focused with a high amount of *Popular Yellow* and/or *Peaceful Green*.

Think about all the key people in your life ......... your partner, family members, friends and those at work. Identify each one's main style and go back and read the chapter about their main style. Start to understand what they like and dislike. Think about how they behave in ways similar to you or completely different.

# 9. Upsets, Arguments and Fights

Why do we have upsets and arguments with others, especially the people we love and care about most in the world?

It's just because we have different personalities, different ways of looking at things.

In any situation we may react differently, which can cause other people to get cross or upset.

Understanding each others' personality will not change the way you look at things, but it helps to know the reason why. You can then decide how to react.

Much of behaviour is habit. Like having a messy car filled with empty drink bottles, various items of clothing and last week's crisp packets. Not very important to the people-focused *Popular Yellow* and *Peaceful Green* types but this will make the *Powerful Red* and *Perfect Blue* very annoyed. Being tidy and cleaning up is a habit that can be cultivated by *Popular Yellow* and *Peaceful Green* in order to please their *Powerful Red* and *Perfect Blue* family members. Being people-focused is not an excuse to live in a mess.

Similarly, the *Powerful Red* and *Perfect Blue* individuals can choose to overlook some untidiness to make their *Popular Yellow* and *Peaceful Green* family members happy. Being meticulous and ultra-tidy is also a habit.

Harmonious relationships happen when both parties make adjustments to their behaviour because the relationship is important to them.

Upsets and Arguments happen because of communication - the way we talk, what we talk about, how much we talk, how freely or clearly, we express ourselves.

Communication style is directly related to your main style of personality.

Different styles focus on, and talk about, different things.

It has already been mentioned that the *Powerful Red* and *Perfect Blue* will talk about work, events and things, while the *Popular Yellow* and *Peaceful Green* talk mostly about family, friends and the people involved.

There are differences in how much each style talks and how well each listen.

*Popular Yellow* talk a lot but aren't good listeners, whereas *Peaceful Green* are excellent listeners but only talk if they feel safe and secure.

*Powerful Red* and *Perfect Blue* tend to talk only when they have something important or meaningful to say. The *Powerful Red* will be brief and to the point but the *Perfect Blue* will go into great detail.

# 10. COMMUNICATION

## *Powerful Red* Communication…. Think Controlling

These are probably the easiest people to recognise as their voice and presence seems to dominate the space.

They are direct in their approach and always in a hurry so this can come across as abrupt. They are just not interested in the detail and will interrupt you to get to the point quicker. The *Powerful Red* knows what they want and they just want you to get on with it. They usually take control of the conversation.

And another thing – they'll be doing other things while they are talking to you – especially if you are on the phone.

## *Popular Yellow* Communication …. Think Talkative

These people are also easy to recognise. In a room full of people, they will be the one doing lots of talking, telling stories and surrounded by others.

The *Popular Yellow* talks much faster than other people, with a lively tone and the voice has lots of inflection in it. They love talking. They talk for pleasure. Conversations can be long as they tend to give lots of detail, jump from one thing to another and they also use exciting extravagant words like "amazing" or "awesome".

They are not good listeners because they want to tell you about their experiences, not listen to yours so they will often interrupt you. If you are having a conversation with someone and a *Popular Yellow* person joins you, notice that they take over the conversation.

## *Peaceful Green* Communication …. Think Agreeable

The *Peaceful Green* is harder to identify because they don't talk freely until they are comfortable with you. In a room full of people, the *Peaceful Green* styles are the ones listening to everyone else. They are the best listeners because they are genuinely interested in others. They listen before talking. We think of them as agreeable because they won't argue with you, even if they disagree with your point of view, they keep their opinions and emotions hidden.

You will notice a warm, pleasant gentleness about the *Peaceful Green* person. They are soft spoken with a slower pace and often use words like "feel, together, family".

## *Perfect Blue* Communication …. Think Questioning

You can recognise a *Perfect Blue* person because their conversation is very business-like. It's direct, precise and to the point. You might think they are a bit abrupt because they just ask questions, often bluntly.

There is very little voice inflection. It's a more serious, formal tone. There are long pauses because the *Perfect Blue* needs to think before speaking. No matter how much you are tempted (if you are *Powerful Red* or *Popular Yellow*) don't jump in, let the *Perfect Blue* think.

The *Perfect Blue* individual often enunciates their words. This allows them to slow down the pace of the discussion and analyse whatever you are saying. They will try to think ahead of you so that they are prepared for discussions.

# 11. EMOTIONS

There are also differences in how each style expresses their thoughts and feelings.

## *Powerful Red* Emotions ....

The *Powerful Red* keeps their feelings under control but they will get impatient. You'll notice this. They do have sudden outbursts of emotion. This is because they have a short fuse and their direct response to conflict is to explode with an outburst of anger. And when the *Powerful Red* is angry they get very angry and everyone knows about it. They put everyone in their place with this outburst. Then for the *Powerful Red* the situation is over, forgotten. They do not realise that they may have upset the gentler styles.

## *Popular Yellow* Emotions ....

The *Popular Yellow* is very emotional, like a roller coaster ride. Mostly you'll see the *Popular Yellow* person as bubbly and cheerful but they have mood swings. Their lows are low and they let you know all about it. Fortunately, it doesn't last very long. Another emotion of the *Popular Yellow* is that they are extremely optimistic so they always think the impossible can be done. When this is not achieved the other styles respond. *Powerful Red* with anger, *Peaceful Green* and *Perfect Blue* with upset, disappointment and lack of trust.

## *Peaceful Green* Emotions ....

The *Peaceful Green* individual is quite emotional as well, but unlike the *Popular Yellow*, they do not show it, they hide their feelings. They keep any thoughts or grievances to themselves until it all gets too much and then they walk off. They leave. They leave their home or work completely surprising everyone else. For the *Peaceful Green* conflict is difficult. Because they are easy and relaxed they tend to let others have their way to keep the peace. They don't tell anyone how they are feeling. They bottle things up. Every now and then they explode with an outburst that surprises everyone. However, they will open up with people they trust.

## Perfect Blue Emotions ....

The *Perfect Blue* is very controlled with their emotions. However, they suffer from mood swings. They have high and low moods. In fact, the lows can be very gloomy. It's as if a black cloud has entered the room. When they feel angry or frustrated they tend to cut themselves off from other people. They become withdrawn and distant. They avoid conflict with the silent treatment or they'll go off on their own.

Our communication and our moods affect all our relationships. Become more aware of your own communication and emotional style. Identify how it differs from the style of your partner, friend or colleague.

If the relationship is important to you, discuss your differences. Decide on the changes to behaviour that are necessary for the relationship to work.

# 12. PERSONAL RELATIONSHIPS

You are probably reading this book because you want some help with a particular relationship. Let's look more closely at the different relationships you might have.

**Personal relationships like marriage and partnerships.**

I am not a guidance or marriage counsellor so I cannot give you advice about your personal relationships. Instead, what this book does is discuss behaviour patterns and how the understanding of the differences in our personality can help you have better personal relationships. The aim is to give you tools to start improving areas you'd like to change.

Is your relationship based on opposites being attracted to each other?

Opposite qualities enhance a relationship because each brings different strengths to that relationship and we can learn to play to each other's strengths.

It's also about choice. Let's say your partner is very untidy (they are a ***Popular Yellow***) and you are fastidious (you are a ***Perfect Blue***). You have the choice …. you can tidy up after them because it's important to you, not them, or leave the mess because it's their way and not get bothered by it. Or there is another choice…you could talk about it and reach some compromise.

What you can't do is change somebody else. We can change our own behaviour any time we choose, but we can't change somebody else's.

The other person's strengths attract us.

The other person's weaknesses annoy us.

A *Peaceful Green* will be attracted to the assertiveness and decisiveness of the *Powerful Red* but at times this characteristic will upset the *Peaceful Green*. This is because the *Peaceful Green* partner is peace-loving and agreeable. They may feel the *Powerful Red* person is pushing them around.

Similarly, the *Popular Yellow* is a great conversationalist but disorganised. The *Perfect Blue* is not very sociable but highly organised. These two will be attracted to each other forming a relationship which completes the whole, so to speak. There will be times though, when these opposite characteristics will annoy each other.

And another thing to remember is that your strong point, taken to extreme, can become a weakness.

For instance, if you are a *Powerful Red* you are dominant, always the leader, but this behaviour at times can be too much and the other styles will think of you as bossy and sometimes a bully.

If you are a *Popular Yellow*, you can dominate conversations with your natural exuberance and talkativeness and the other styles will get annoyed that you don't listen or let them speak.

The *Peaceful Green* strength is your calmness and keeping everything as it should be, but this calmness can irritate others who would like you to show more excitement and energy.

And for the *Perfect Blue*, your strength is your meticulous attention to detail which when taken too far will come across to the other styles as too fussy and slow.

So how do you use your knowledge of people's behaviour and personality to help you in a relationship?

**Know, understand and accept the two basic differences between styles.**

- The pace at which they approach things. *Powerful Red* & *Popular Yellows* are fast paced while *Peaceful Green* & *Perfect Blues* prefer a slower pace.
- What they focus on. *Powerful Red* & *Perfect Blues* focus on tasks and *Popular Yellow* & *Peaceful Greens* focus on people

**Know and understand your strengths and weaknesses.**

*Powerful Red* is strong willed and an organiser but can be insensitive and inconsiderate.

*Popular Yellow* is enthusiastic and spontaneous but can be undisciplined and disorganised.

*Peaceful Green* is patient and peaceful but can be indecisive and compromising.

*Perfect Blue* is self-disciplined and serious but can be critical and moody.

# Do you have a blind spot?

A blind spot is that part of your behaviour or personality that you have forgotten about or choose to ignore. Your blind spot is when you don't recognise the impact your behaviour is having on others. It is important to recognise which of our actions impact others positively, and which have a negative effect on a person with a different style.

Listen to the feedback others are giving you. It may be subtle like their body language, facial expressions or the attention they are paying you. Or it might be outright with statements like "you're driving me crazy" or the other person becomes very quiet or storms off. Be sensitive to your impact on others.

You need to recognise when you need to modify your behaviour. By this I mean ask yourself the question "How important is this?" Many arguments occur over trivial things where both parties think their opinion is more important.

One thing that can help enormously is making the distinction between the Facts versus the Opinions or Stories we create around those facts.

Example: Tidying up the kitchen after dinner. The Fact is it needs to be tidied. The Opinion is when.

The *Perfect Blue* cook will want it tidied as soon as possible (and as they cook they clean up after themselves anyway). The *Popular Yellow* partner will say they will do it later, when they have finished talking to.... (friend, family member or work mate) but they often forget because other fun things get in the way.

Each person's opinion is correct. But is it worth an argument?

**Perfect Blue** cook can accept the mess a little bit longer, in other words make a small adjustment to their behaviour of wanting everything to be perfect and orderly. Or **Popular Yellow** partner could change their behaviour and clean the kitchen before the fun. Or they both agree that **Popular Yellow** partner will tidy up later but if this is the agreement **Popular Yellow** partner must keep their word and do it when they say they will. Later implies that night not later that week! And **Perfect Blue** cook must not allow themselves to clean it anyway rather than waiting.

By understanding your strengths and weaknesses you can make a decision in any situation whether or not it's best to change your behaviour slightly in order to get on better with the other person. It is a conscious choice you make at any point in time.

Know and understand your partner's strengths and weaknesses.

Similarly, when you recognise your partner's behaviour is just part of their personality style it seems to help diffuse any tension. That's the way they are because of this characteristic or that behaviour. It's most helpful when both people in the relationship use the **Personality** tool.

Each of the four styles sees the world differently.

The disorganised **Popular Yellow** will see the **Perfect Blue** as fussy and picky while the meticulous **Perfect Blue** will see the **Popular Yellow** as a messy individual.

In a relationship the **Powerful Red** & **Popular Yellow**s want to make decisions quickly, whether it's what to choose from the restaurant menu or which house to buy. The ***Peaceful Green*** & ***Perfect Blue***s want to think about it, read the entire menu and weigh up the choices or research thoroughly all aspects of the property.

If planning a holiday, ***Powerful Red*** & ***Perfect Blue***s will focus on the where, what and how of the location, accommodation etc whereas the ***Popular Yellow*** & ***Peaceful Green***s will focus on the who …who else can come too or will be there, what is there for the children to do.

Is one better than the other?

There are advantages and disadvantages.

For instance, the ***Powerful Red*** & ***Popular Yellow*** might not make the best property decisions by being too hasty. The ***Peaceful Green*** & ***Perfect Blue*** might miss out on the best deals because of their need to reflect. And the reverse is also true…. ***Powerful Red*** & ***Popular Yellow*** can pick up great deals because they act fast and ***Peaceful Green*** & ***Perfect Blue*** will avoid costly mistakes by not rushing into decisions.

Remember your partner's strengths.

These are the qualities that attracted you in the first place. Acknowledge these. Give approval, compliment and appreciate these qualities.

# 13. RELATIONSHIPS WITH CHILDREN

## Young children

My observations of young children suggest that at a very early age the characteristics of their main styles can be observed.

Your child may build a tower of blocks or complete a puzzle with a lot of intensity and focus and then once it's done be bored with that activity. That's **Powerful Red** behaviour. This child is likely to be quite demanding and definite about what they want to do, where they must go and what they eat.

If your child always wants to play with other children and they don't like being alone that's typical **Popular Yellow** behaviour. This child is a happy laughing child.

Does your child love playing with blocks and want to build a tower over and over again? This child enjoys the security and satisfaction of completing a known task…typical **Peaceful Green** behaviour. The child is likely to be gentle and enjoy playing with their toys.

Perhaps your child gets frustrated when colouring in. They think the end result doesn't look good enough, isn't perfect. Or they may spend ages completing it. That's **Perfect Blue** behaviour. This child will be quite content with their own company.

Although children may demonstrate certain behavioural style characteristics, as they grow these may stay the same or they may change.

Lots of factors are involved in children's development …. family circumstances, place in the family, friendships, school environment to name a few.

Children need to grow, change and develop their own personality.

## Teenagers

If you have teenagers you have probably recognised their main personality style or styles by now.

In the classroom it is easy to recognise the main styles.

The *Powerful Red* teenager is often controlling, of their parents, siblings, teachers and friends. This is the leader of a group or gang. They get bored very easily with school work and hate repetitive activities or giving detail in their answers, although they do like to solve problems. Their assertiveness means they will stand up to teachers and argue, which gets them into trouble.

The *Popular Yellow* teenager is talkative and also a leader of a group because they are popular amongst their peers. They are easily distracted from their school work as they prefer to chatter and have fun with their friends. They have an abundance of charisma and can charm their teachers.

The *Peaceful Green* teenager is agreeable, getting on with other students and the teachers. Kind, devoted friends, they work well in groups and always want to help others, including their teachers.

The *Perfect Blue* teenager is conscientious, often intense, but always highly organised. Their books are neat & tidy and they strive to complete perfect work. They always, always obey the school rules.

Teenagers are influenced by lots of things and peer pressure is a significant one. During the teenage years behaviour can change. Well, that is, the behaviour that we see. Big shifts occur in teenagers' behaviour because they change for particular situations. The teenager may be quiet and well behaved at home but rebel at school by being noisy and argumentative. Or the alternative happens, your son or daughter is difficult to manage at home but the teachers say they are well behaved and hard working at school.

The teenager adopts the behaviour they've decided they want for that situation…. And it's often to do with the peer group…to be seen to be more powerful or popular, or not appear so quiet or conscientious.

## Parents

As parents, our main style of behaviour comes through.

### The *Powerful Red* Parent

Often described as **The Boss**, these parents are determined, hard working, competitive, and energetic. *Powerful Red* parents are often busy parents, with lots of tasks and activities. They focus on problem solving and big picture solutions, and less on the emotions behind something or the reasons why…They do not respond well to dramatic or emotional displays. The *Powerful Red* parent will strive to be a figure of authority and a good role-model for their children. However, if their authority is challenged or they feel disrespected or taken advantage of, they will probably display strong tone and body language.

**Something for *Powerful Red* Parents to think about**…. especially with older children. If your child is also a *Powerful Red*, there may be a struggle for power. It's best to assert your authority early, but allow your child to make some decisions for them self. This still gives them some control over their own lives, which they crave. With *Popular Yellow*, *Peaceful Green*, and *Perfect Blue* children, you will need to be mindful of your tone and body language, as these styles will easily feel rejected or intimidated and may withdraw or avoid you as a result.

**The *Popular Yellow* Parent**

**The Communicator.** Since the *Popular Yellow* focuses on people these parents are great fun, energetic and communicative. They naturally love to be the centre of attention and are happiest when their children are smiling, laughing and interacting with them. Because the *Popular Yellow* parent fears rejection they want to be accepted by their children and the children's friends. This can cause problems when disciplining their child or saying "no". The *Popular Yellow* parent may not be particularly well organised and struggle with time management. Be aware of this if this is you as children can get into trouble if late for school, sports events or appointments through no fault of their own.

**Something for *Popular Yellow* Parents to think about**: You don't really like rules and structure but you should set some for your children while they are growing up and learning. Your *Powerful Red* and *Perfect Blue* children are task-focused so talk to them about their activities rather than the people involved in their lives.

**The *Peaceful Green* Parent**

**The Nurturer.** The parent who provides their children with a stable, calm environment. As parents, they are patient and loyal, putting their family's needs ahead of their own in order to create happy relationships and a peaceful environment. They provide a strong sense of security and grounding for their children. The *Peaceful Green* avoids conflict with others as it causes them a lot of stress which they keep contained. As well, because they don't like change they can be quite stubborn or inflexible.

**Something for the *Peaceful Green* Parent to think about**: You will need to make an effort with your *Powerful Red* child to stand your ground in discipline matters. You, naturally, want to avoid conflict and will be tempted to give in but your *Powerful Red* child will respect you for setting the boundaries. Also, take some time for yourself as well as caring for your family.

The *Perfect Blue* Parent

**The Organiser**. Because they are task-orientated and logical these parents put systems in place around the home for things to run smoothly, but can become quite inflexible when it comes to changing routines. Like the *Peaceful Green* parent, the *Perfect Blue* parent also avoids conflict. At these times, they can become withdrawn and family members will have a difficult time getting close to them. Also, the *Perfect Blue* parent teaches their children to gather information and research thoroughly before coming to a decision.

**Something for a *Perfect Blue* parent to think about**: Because you are very thorough and seek perfection you expect others to be so too. Try not to be too critical of others. With your *Powerful Red* children, you need to assert yourself and set the boundaries. With your people-oriented *Popular Yellow* and *Peaceful Green* children try to be more open and sharing in your communication so they don't feel you are distant from them.

# 14. WORKING RELATIONSHIPS

If you work then this is a chapter for you.

## The Employer or Manager….

If you are an employee, this information will help you understand the management style of your employer, manager or boss. It'll help you because you will understand why they do and say the things they do.

If you are the employer or manager, read this chapter because this is how your employees see you.

### The *Powerful Red* Employer or Manager

The *Powerful Red* employer is assertive and dynamic, always driving towards new goals. They are direct in their manner of speaking which others can find intimidating or insensitive. It may seem like a personal attack to the other styles but it is not meant that way. The *Powerful Red* boss just tells it like it is to them.

The *Powerful Red* boss is always in a hurry and expects immediate action from others. The slower-paced quieter styles, *Peaceful Green* and *Perfect Blue* don't have this same sense of urgency and can get flustered as a result.

The *Powerful Red* boss is a multitasker. Because they do several things at once it may seem difficult to get their attention. You want them to stop and listen to you but they won't. You need to be brief and amazing.

Know your stuff. If they are rushing off somewhere, walk with them to discuss whatever it is.

If you have a new idea or suggestion for the business, sow the seed of it first by just mentioning it and leaving it with them. The *Powerful Red* boss can then think about it and if it's a good suggestion they will announce it, as if they thought of it themselves. That way, they won't feel they are losing control. You know it was your idea and that's all that matters really.

Another way to get the *Powerful Red* boss's attention is to mention your idea but then quickly say it wouldn't work. The *Powerful Red* loves a challenge and you've just offered them one.

**The Popular Yellow Employer or Manager**

If your boss is a *Popular Yellow* you'll find them approachable and easy to talk to. But this also means you will be involved in many meetings, also socials and parties. The *Popular Yellow* boss is likely to instigate recognition programmes for their employees.

One of the disadvantages of the *Popular Yellow* boss is that they are not very good listeners so they can tend to dominate meetings. To get their attention you need to emphasise how your idea or proposal will have a positive impact for other people.

Great motivators, the *Popular Yellow* individuals will get others excited and carry them along with their optimism. If you are a *Perfect Blue* you might find this sort of enthusiasm and fast pace a bit reckless.

The *Popular Yellow* boss is an innovator but not particularly good at planning and organising. They tend to over-promise, and under-deliver. It can be helpful if you write a plan for them with target completion dates.

**The Peaceful Green Employer or Manager**

The characteristics of the *Peaceful Green* are that they are kind & considerate employers. They are very supportive of the people they manage and like to create a relaxed family atmosphere and a very pleasant place to work.

The pace will be slow with very little ever changing. If you are a faster paced person like a *Powerful Red* or *Popular Yellow* you may get frustrated with the time it takes the *Peaceful Green* boss to implement changes.

Because the *Peaceful Green* boss is a great negotiator, you will find them easy to talk to. They will listen carefully and genuinely want to help you. However, although they are very approachable they do not like arguments or disagreements.

**The Perfect Blue Employer or Manager**

The *Perfect Blue* employer is concerned with quality and accuracy. They want and expect perfect products and results. This can place great demands on employees and can take its toll on staff turnover.

The *Perfect Blue* boss does not like interruptions or surprises so if you need to discuss something, schedule an appointment to see them. They are not risk takers so do not expect them to answer or make a decision on the spot. If you are a *Powerful Red* or *Popular Yellow* type you will find this frustrating. Be prepared with all the correct figures and paperwork in order. Leave it with them for them to study. The **Perfect Blue** boss needs time to reflect and will examine the long-range outcomes of your proposals. But they will get back to you.

A business run by a **Perfect Blue** individual will have detailed operating procedures and systems in place that you'll need to follow. They do find delegating difficult. They worry that others won't meet their very high standards so they'll check your work until they are satisfied you meet their requirements. Sometimes they prefer to do things themselves to be sure to get it correct.

## The Employee......

### The Powerful Red Employee...

This employee works best when given lots of challenges. This is what motivates them. They need a variety of work so that they don't get bored. Provide them with exciting opportunities to advance their career. The **Powerful Red** employee loves working under the pressure of time restraints. They don't like to feel they are being controlled or supervised. They need to feel they are in control of the people around them and their environment. Give them independent work and assign them responsibility for directing others. Create competitions and chances to win. Acknowledge their results, successes and the impact on the bottom line with rewards. Give them compliments for tangible things, the big results not all the steps along the way.

And as with all things in dealing with a *Powerful Red*, be brief and direct. You'll always get direct answers from the *Powerful Red* employee but don't expect any small talk.

**The Popular Yellow Employee**

As the *Popular Yellow* is gregarious they need lots of people contact. They need to work with others not by themselves. In an office situation, they work best in open-plan where they can talk to others. They like to entertain with stories of what they have done or are going to do. Work for them is a very social place so they also like social activities outside of work hours.

The *Popular Yellow* employee likes to have their ideas heard. They don't like lots of detail but they do like others to listen to their ideas. They need recognition of any achievements and enjoy being the centre of attention in a public announcement rather than the more private thank you card that a *Peaceful Green* or *Perfect Blue* employee would enjoy.

The enthusiasm of the *Popular Yellow* employee is infectious which makes them a natural at motivating others in the team. They are also very creative when solving problems because of their ability to think outside the box.

**The Peaceful Green Employee**

Your *Peaceful Green* employee is your reliable, dependable and loyal worker who is motivated by a desire to help others. They enjoy working and cooperating in small groups where there is no conflict. They need clear instructions about what you want done and how you want it done. Compared to the *Powerful Red* and *Popular Yellow*, the *Peaceful Green* worker needs more support from their boss. They are respectful towards their employer.

The *Peaceful Green* employee works at their own pace but they need stability and a predictable environment. If changes are inevitable it is best to tell the *Peaceful Green* what to expect so they have time to prepare.

They do like to feel appreciated for the effort they put into their work. This is where a thoughtfully worded thank you card means a lot. They need to be thanked often, genuinely, personally and in private for their cooperation & loyalty. Where the *Popular Yellow* loves being recognised in public the *Peaceful Green* employee would be quite embarrassed.

Although *Peaceful Green* employees do not like any conflict in their own lives they are often good at reconciling conflicts between others because they are patient and good listeners. In the workplace, they often take the role of peace-maker.

*Peaceful Green* employees will step into leadership situations if asked to. The difficulties occur if there are any out-going *Powerful Red* or *Popular Yellow* people in the team who tend to dominate discussions. In this situation, the *Peaceful Green* employee feels overpowered and clams up. Competitiveness, aggression or confrontation is de-motivating for the *Peaceful Green* individual.

**The Perfect Blue Employee**

The *Perfect Blue* employee prefers to work alone so ideally, they need their own office. If that's not possible they at least need their own desk.

Privacy is important to them allowing them to think, plan, prepare, evaluate and problem solve before sharing the material with others.

They like to be in a situation where they are the expert, performing technical or specialised work which is respected by others. They are the ideal employee to be given the task of proof reading any article or proposal. However, they need adequate time to complete a task. The *Perfect Blue* hates last minute panics or impossible deadlines. They want their work completed perfectly, and therefore take longer to do so. If they feel they have insufficient time to complete a task the *Perfect Blue* worker will lose their motivation. The faster-paced *Powerful Red* and *Popular Yellow* can get frustrated with the time it takes the *Perfect Blue* worker and this need for perfection.

*Perfect Blue* workers analyse a project thoroughly from every aspect, assessing every detail. Other styles might think the *Perfect Blue* employee is a bit sceptical but they are just considering every conceivable outcome.

*Perfect Blue* employees do work well in small groups where they form close relationships. They are even-tempered employees and like other people to concentrate on logic not emotion in the workplace. When there is an argument or any type of conflict the *Perfect Blue* worker will avoid others all day. They'll take their lunch break working at their desk or they'll go out of the workplace altogether, perhaps for a walk.

# 15. Individual Partnerships

In this section, you will find a guide to individual pairings of styles. Use it to understand each of the relationships you have.

For instance, if you are a *Peaceful Green* and your partner is mainly *Perfect Blue* read the *Peaceful Green* and *Perfect Blue* page.

If your boss is *Powerful Red* then read the *Powerful Red* and *Peaceful Green* page.

If you have 2 main styles e.g. *Perfect Blue* and *Peaceful Green* and your partner is a *Powerful Red* you will need to read the pairing of *Powerful Red* with *Perfect Blue* and *Powerful Red* with *Peaceful Green*.

There is plenty of room on each page to make notes about the partnerships you have within your family, with friends or in the workplace.

## Two *Powerful Reds*

Both of you have an assertive, direct style and want to dominate the relationship, be the controlling person. Because you have similar strengths you also respect each other. However, you both prefer to work in your own way to find solutions to problems rather than cooperatively. You are both motivated by being in control, having challenges and rewards. You like to be admired by others for your strengths and abilities to achieve results quickly.

*Powerful Red*s are considered to be risk-takers which is a good thing for entrepreneurial success. You both prefer to act rather than consider strategies. Depending on the circumstances you may need to rein in each other before a situation gets out of control.

The main area to watch out for is when either of you is under pressure. Your natural response to pressure is to dictate. This isn't going to work with two *Powerful Red*s. The outcome of two people dictating to each other will be open conflict, shouting etc.

Conflict may arise when you both want to be in control. A solution to this is to take on different roles or projects. Divide something up and share out the tasks. Each be in charge of something different.

For instance, if you are planning a holiday together, one could be in charge of the flights etc while the other looks after accommodation. Alternatively, one organises the holiday this year, the other the next year. You can relax knowing the other will complete the task well.

You are both very competitive, wanting to win or be the best. This is another area where you could have conflict. Try to compete with other people rather than each other.

Two *Popular Yellows*

Because you are both out-going, sociable and communicative you will get on really well. Every day will be full of fun and noise. There will be lots of open expressions of love as each of you needs to feel liked and admired.

Sometimes there might be some light-hearted competition for the attention of others but it is nothing serious.

Something for each partner to be aware of are the highs and lows that *Popular Yellow* types suffer from. The emotional highs are exciting and much talked about. Similarly, the lows are low and everyone hears about them but fortunately the lows don't last long.

Under pressure *Popular Yellow* people tend to have outbursts of anger but it's all over very quickly, forgotten about and no grudges held.

***Powerful Red*** with ***Popular Yellow***

Here we have a complimentary relationship of the ***Powerful Red*** who focuses on material and business success with the ***Popular Yellow*** whose interests are around social success.

You are both are confident and out-going. There will be lots of energy in your relationship.

One area that will cause some issues is the ***Popular Yellow***'s extroverted nature and the need for approval and attention. The ***Powerful Red*** finds these things unnecessary and focuses on just getting something done. The ***Popular Yellow*** partner should work on not being so needy of attention. The ***Powerful Red*** partner should try to show their caring side more.

When there is conflict, the ***Popular Yellow*** response is to attack while the ***Powerful Red*** dictates. This situation can be verbally explosive. Each partner needs to control this behaviour to keep the peace. Ask yourself "how important is it that I'm right in this situation?"

Two *Peaceful Green*s

Because you are both, patient, loyal and dependable, this relationship will be long and steady. Each of you will care for and support the other.

One problem to be aware of is the tendency of both of you to resist change and so nothing ever changes. If a change must be made like buying a house it can take a very long time to finalise because both individuals need time to adjust and decide. One solution is to set a deadline for a decision to be made.

If a situation arises where the two of you are placed under some stress it will be very difficult for you both. The one with the higher amount of *Powerful Red* mixed in with the *Peaceful Green* will need to take control.

### *Powerful Red* with *Peaceful Green*

These two styles are complete opposites. *Powerful Red* is out-going, louder and focuses on results whereas *Peaceful Green* is reserved, quieter and interested mostly in people. Together they provide variety and value in a family or team environment.

*Powerful Red* individuals will get frustrated and irritated with the slower pace and reluctance to change of the *Peaceful Green* partner. Similarly, *Peaceful Green* partner will get upset with the other's assertiveness which will come across as bossy and the risk-taking which will seem foolish.

The most important thing for these individuals to do is to respect each other's strengths that they bring to the relationship and recognise they are providing something that they themselves don't have.

For a successful relationship, the *Powerful Red* partner must work on their people skills and show the *Peaceful Green* patience, love and consideration. They want your leadership and direction but without the domination. They also need to know you care. The *Peaceful Green* needs to express their feelings and not bottle things up inside. When asked what you want, develop confidence to say what you mean.

*Popular Yellow* with *Peaceful Green*

The nature of these two styles will complement each other, generally forming a successful relationship. The out-going bubbly *Popular Yellow* will offset the quieter more reserved *Peaceful Green*. Conversely, the steady dependable *Peaceful Green* will counteract the overly optimistic and energetic *Popular Yellow*.

Both partners need to appreciate these differences. One is urgent and fast-paced while the other is steady and patient. There is a time and place for both.

Because both are people focussed, they are not good at organising something that requires detail. This means that to get things done, particularly very important decisions, will require the *Popular Yellow* partner to assume control. Something to watch out for is that the *Peaceful Green* partner may become quite dependent on the more assertive *Popular Yellow* partner. Over time this may lead to either or both of you feeling resentful.

Two *Perfect Blue*s

Here we have two individuals who share a concern for accuracy and like things around them to be perfect. Neither of you are risk-takers. You both follow the rules and will establish systems for the smooth running of the home or workplace.

You are not usually competitive by nature but when together you can become competitive around your skills or knowledge. Each one of you wanting to be better than the other and this may cause disagreements.

Because this style is not people-focused, neither of you can express your feelings freely. In times of stress the *Perfect Blue* person withdraws, becomes distant. This can be a problem if both of you behave like this. No communication might create resentment. It takes practice but both of you can learn to share your feelings and keep communication open.

### *Powerful Red* with *Perfect Blue*

These two styles have a lot in common in that they are both task-focused. You concentrate on practical matters and achieving your goals rather than social interaction.

Challenges however, may arise from your differences. The *Powerful Red* partner is demanding and direct whereas the *Perfect Blue* partner is usually more subtle and diplomatic. Also, the *Perfect Blue* has a need for precision and accuracy whereas the *Powerful Red* just wants the job done well but fast.

Neither the *Powerful Red* nor the *Perfect Blue* are people-orientated so neither is fully aware of the other person's feelings. When there is a disagreement the *Powerful Red* partner will dictate which will do no good as the *Perfect Blue* partner's response to pressure is to withdraw, go off on their own or be silent. The *Powerful Red* partner needs to lower the dominance factor and show patience. The *Perfect Blue* partner needs to act with more confidence, to gain respect, and explain what's wrong, clearly but as briefly as possible.

*Popular Yellow* with *Perfect Blue*

These two styles are considerably different. The effervescent *Popular Yellow* is focused on happy relationships while the cautious *Perfect Blue* is focused on getting things done and done right. Because you are opposites you are attracted to each other, in fact you complement each other well, but the differences can lead to conflict.

The *Popular Yellow* partner will get impatient and irritated with the *Perfect Blue* partner's need to check everything before going ahead.

The *Perfect Blue* partner will get upset and find it frustrating because the *Popular Yellow* partner does not give any regard to practical issues.

This can be an unpredictable relationship. Both individuals need to remain aware of their differences and notice when this is having a detrimental effect on the relationship. If this happens you both need to adapt your styles to be more like the other.

***Peaceful Green*** with ***Perfect Blue***

This is a relationship formed by two reserved individuals who depend on mutual trust and understanding. It is a good working relationship because both are concerned with care and accuracy.

Difficulties may arise in the area of communication when one or the other of you is under stress. Neither wants confrontation or to cause offence. As a result, neither of you will express your feelings.

The ***Peaceful Green*** keeps their feelings locked up inside for a long time until they can't cope and then they up and leave (the marriage or workplace) without warning.

The ***Perfect Blue*** doesn't express their feelings either. Instead they withdraw and stop talking until they have got over the issue.

In this combination of personalities both of you must make an effort to alter your style and communicate your feelings and desires with the other.

# A Final Word

The *Powerful Red*. You need to be aware of when your assertive dominance is adversely affecting others. They won't like your bossiness, your insistence that you are right. At any time only, you can decide if you really need to behave in such an assertive way. Notice when it's a good time to ask others for their opinions rather than dictating.

The *Popular Yellow*. It is your decision how much to dominate a conversation. At any time, you can stop talking and take an interest in others by asking them questions. Listen to their answers without jumping in with your own story to tell. Don't disappoint others by setting unrealistic goals with your wonderful optimistic take on things. Keep your word.

The *Peaceful Green*. Remember there are times when you miss out on the fun by not being more spontaneous. Everything in the world is changing, choose wisely and enjoy the changes. Don't take things to heart. People love you for the gentle caring person you are, so open up to them more.

The *Perfect Blue*. Recognise when perfect is important but good enough is fine too. Other people don't necessarily appreciate the accuracy and detail in tasks that you do. When you're with a *Popular Yellow* or *Powerful Red* you need to speed up your actions and speech.

So often people use the strong aspect of their personality as an excuse for their behaviour.

Wrong.

Our behaviour is simply that...behaviour. There are good people and bad people with every combination of styles.

At any moment, you can choose to change your behaviour. That's over to you. It boils down to how important that particular relationship is to you.

Understand the differences and strengths of each individual in your life and use the knowledge of your own personality to enjoy your relationships.

Wishing you lots of success and happiness in all your relationships.

# About the Author

Beverly Kepple is the owner of Coaching 4 Business (UK) Ltd and Lots of Success, a business providing behavioural profiles and training using the DISC system.

For the past 15 years Beverly has trained business owners and individuals in the use of the DISC tool, in particular making the best use of their strengths and being aware of their limitations. Her clients are international; United Kingdom, Ireland, United States, Australia and New Zealand.

Beverly is passionate about helping people be happy and achieve their full potential.

Her first book, "DISCovering the Ultimate Tool" was written to help business owners and coaches.

Beverly spent a good part of her life in New Zealand but now lives in England with her husband Lindsay, close to their three daughters and their families.

Beverly can be contacted via the website www.lots-of-success.com

www.ingramcontent.com/pod-product-compliance
Lightning Source LLC
Chambersburg PA
CBHW071848020426
42331CB00007B/1910